FUN FACT FILE: FIERCE FISH!

20 FUN FACTS ABOUT
BARRACUDAS

By Heather Moore Niver

Gareth Stevens
Publishing

Please visit our website, www.garethstevens.com. For a free color catalog of all our high-quality books, call toll free 1-800-542-2595 or fax 1-877-542-2596.

Library of Congress Cataloging-in-Publication Data

Niver, Heather Moore.
20 fun facts about barracudas / Heather Moore Niver.
    p. cm. — (Fun fact file: fierce fish!)
Includes index.
ISBN 978-1-4339-6976-8 (pbk.)
ISBN 978-1-4339-6977-5 (6-pack)
ISBN 978-1-4339-6975-1 (library binding)
1. Barracudas—Juvenile literature. I. Title. II. Title: Twenty fun facts about barracudas.
QL638.S77N58 2012
597'.7—dc23

                                     2011048254

First Edition

Published in 2013 by
Gareth Stevens Publishing
111 East 14th Street, Suite 349
New York, NY 10003

Designer: Ben Gardner
Editor: Greg Roza

Photo credits: Cover, pp. 1, 5, 6, 7, 8, 9, 10, 11, 15, 16, 24 Shutterstock.com; p. 14 Steven Hunt/Photographer's Choice/Getty Images; p. 17 David Fleetham/Photographer's Choice/ Getty Images; p. 18 Pete Atkinson/Riser/Getty Images; p. 19 Masa Ushioda/age fotostock/ Getty Images; p. 20 Borat Furlan/WaterFrame/Getty Images; p. 21 Photo Researchers/Photo Researchers/Getty Images; pp. 22, 23 iStockphoto.com; p. 25 Reinhard Dirscherl/WaterFrame/ Getty Images; p. 26 Sami Sarkis/Photographer's Choice/Getty Images; p. 27 Peter Arnold/ Secret Sea Visions/Getty Images; p. 29 Jeffery L. Rotman/Peter Arnold/Getty Images.

Printed in the United States of America

CPSIA compliance information: Batch #CS12GS: For further information contact Gareth Stevens, New York, New York at 1-800-542-2595.

Contents

Words in the glossary appear in **bold** type the first time they are used in the text.

Scary and Speedy

With a bullet-shaped body and a mouth full of supersharp teeth, the barracuda is a scary-looking fish. But there's no reason to stay on the beach. Barracudas don't attack humans—very often.

Barracudas aren't new to Earth's oceans. They've been swimming around for 50 million years. They've had plenty of time to become great hunters. Let's jump into the water and learn more about these speedy fish.

Barracudas are fast fish. The great barracuda can reach speeds around 35 miles (56 km) per hour for short bursts when hunting.

Tiger of the Sea

FACT 1

The barracuda is so beastly it's called "tiger of the sea."

The barracuda may get its name from the Spanish word *barraco*, which means "overlapping tooth." The barracuda's lower jaw sticks out a little, and it has sharp teeth like fangs. This trait has earned the barracuda the nickname "tiger of the sea."

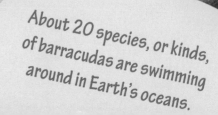

About 20 species, or kinds, of barracudas are swimming around in Earth's oceans.

Sharp Sight

A barracuda's eyes are always open.

Barracudas are fish, which means they're **cold-blooded** animals. They're also **vertebrates**. They have scales all over their bodies and swim with fins. Most fish don't have eyelids, so they can't blink.

Barracudas have yellowish-green eyes.

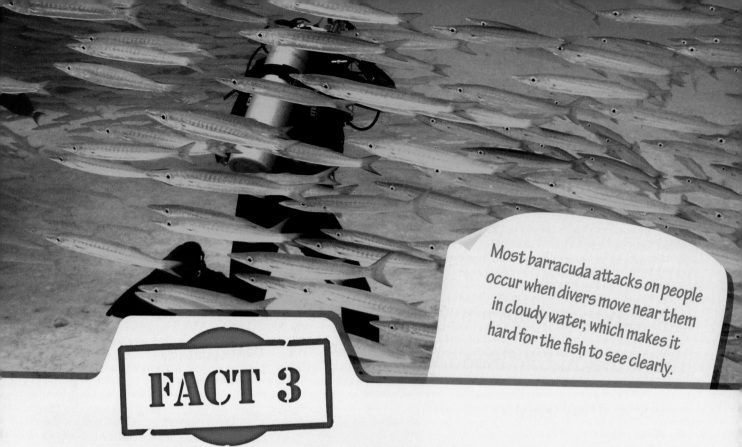

Most barracuda attacks on people occur when divers move near them in cloudy water, which makes it hard for the fish to see clearly.

FACT 3

Barracudas have excellent eyesight.

Barracudas have great vision, which helps with hunting. They'll strike at just about anything moving in the water. Sometimes human swimmers are bitten. However, reports of attacks on humans aren't very common.

Slow-swimming barracudas may actually be asleep.

Because they don't have eyelids, barracudas sleep with their eyes open. If a barracuda seems to be swimming slowly, it may be snoozing. But don't bother it. They're always aware of what's around them, even when taking a nap.

A barracuda will attack quickly if someone bothers it during its nap.

9

FACT 5

The biggest barracudas can weigh 100 pounds (45 kg).

The great barracuda can be as long as 6 feet (1.8 m) and weigh up to 100 pounds (45 kg). But not all barracudas are huge beasts. Some species are not even 1 foot (0.3 m) long.

The average size for barracudas is 3 to 4 feet (0.9 to 1.2 m).

Finding These Fish

Most barracudas live in tropical waters to stay warm.

Barracudas like to swim in warm water. It helps keep these cold-blooded critters warm. They can be found in the warm, **tropical** waters of the Atlantic, the Pacific, and the Indian Oceans. Some barracudas live in slightly cooler, or **temperate**, areas, too.

Barracuda Basics

name	where they are found	longest
Australian barracuda	Indo-Pacific	39 inches (99 cm)
bicuda	southwest Atlantic	18 inches (46 cm)
bigeye barracuda	Indo-Pacific	30 inches (76 cm)
blackfin barracuda	Indo-Pacific	67 inches (170 cm)
European barracuda	eastern Atlantic	65 inches (165 cm)
great barracuda	Indo-Pacific	79 inches (201 cm)
Guachanche barracuda	western Atlantic	79 inches (201 cm)
Guinean barracuda	eastern Atlantic	81 inches (206 cm)
Heller's barracuda	Indian Ocean	31 inches (79 cm)
Japanese barracuda	western Pacific	14 inches (36 cm)
Lucas barracuda	eastern central Pacific	28 inches (71 cm)
Mexican barracuda	eastern Pacific	50 inches (127 cm)
northern sennet	western Atlantic	18 inches (46 cm)

name	where they are found	longest
obtuse barracuda	Indo-Pacific	22 inches (56 cm)
Pacific barracuda	eastern Pacific	57 inches (145 cm)
pelican barracuda	southwest Pacific	36 inches (91 cm)
pickhandle barracuda	Indo-Pacific	59 inches (150 cm)
red barracuda	northwest Pacific	20 inches (51 cm)
sawtooth barracuda	Indo-Pacific	35 inches (89 cm)
sharpfin barracuda	Indo-Pacific	31 inches (79 cm)
southern sennet	western Atlantic	24 inches (61 cm)
Sphyraena iburiensis	northwest Pacific	9 inches (23 cm)
Sphyraena waitii	Indo-Pacific	12 inches (30 cm)
yellowmouth barracuda	eastern central Atlantic	50 inches (127 cm)
yellowstripe barracuda	Indo-Pacific/Mediterranean	12 inches (30 cm)
yellowtail barracuda	Indo-Pacific	24 inches (61 cm)

Chow Down!

FACT 7

Barracudas eat small prey whole and can cut large prey in half with one bite.

When a barracuda spots its **prey**, the prey may have less than a second to live. The barracuda dives forward with open jaws. Its pointed teeth grab the prey. Sawlike teeth act like scissors and cut the prey in half.

A barracuda's fang-like teeth fit into holes in the opposite jaw. This allows the fish to close its mouth.

Barracudas sometimes eat bigger fish, too. They'll even eat other barracudas!

FACT 8

Barracudas hide in sea grass to hunt prey.

Barracudas eat many kinds of small fish, such as snappers, grunts, and mullets. They can easily chase down these fish. However, they sometimes hide and wait for food. They may float in sea grass, wait for prey to swim by, and then attack.

FACT 9

Barracuda bodies are made for fast swimming and tight turns.

Barracudas can follow the quickest fish, even through small spaces. Their bodies are long, but they're also very **flexible**. This means barracudas can easily twist and make tight turns as they follow prey through a **coral reef**.

Sharks and tuna sometimes munch barracuda for lunch.

Adult barracudas are so fast and powerful that they don't have much to worry about. But they do have some **predators**. Sharks, tuna, and goliath groupers are all willing to take on a barracuda in hopes of a tasty meal.

A Caribbean reef shark takes a bite out of an unlucky barracuda.

17

Barracuda Breathing

A barracuda with a wide-open mouth may not be hungry. It might be breathing.

Barracudas need oxygen just like humans, but they don't have lungs. Instead, they have gills, which are slits in the sides of

their head. Like other fish, barracudas get their oxygen by swallowing water and pushing it out over their gills.

A great barracuda swims by a shipwreck near Key Largo, Florida.

FACT 12

Barracudas don't have lungs, but they do have an air-filled organ called a swim bladder.

Barracudas use their fins to swim. However, they have a swim bladder to help them move up and down. This is a sac that holds gas. The barracuda adds gas to its swim bladder to move up and removes gas to move down.

Sleek and Silver

A barracuda's colors help it hide from prey.

Barracudas usually have gray or silver backs. This makes them hard to see to fish swimming above them. Most have a white belly. The tips of their **caudal** fins are white, too. This makes it hard for fish swimming below a barracuda to see it.

The barracuda's long, sleek body also helps it swim fast. This shape is called fusiform.

Lean and Mean

Barracudas have special fins that help them whiz through the water.

The barracuda is sometimes compared to the freshwater **pike.** One big difference is that barracudas have two separate **dorsal** fins. They also have a forked tail. These features are what help barracudas swoosh through the water so fast.

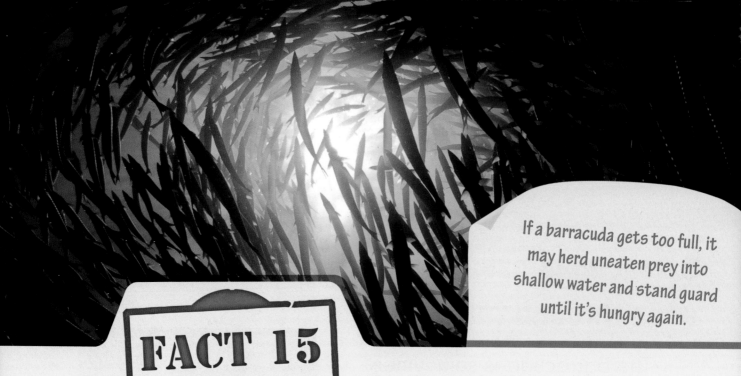

If a barracuda gets too full, it may herd uneaten prey into shallow water and stand guard until it's hungry again.

FACT 15

Barracudas "herd" schools of small fish in order to catch them more easily.

When a barracuda finds a school of small fish, it circles around them, somewhat like a farm dog herding cattle. Soon the frightened fish bunch together. Then the barracuda dives into the group, cutting and biting the fish with its sharp teeth.

Baby Barracudas

FACT 16

Female barracudas can lay up to 300,000 eggs at once.

Female barracudas lay many eggs in deep water. The eggs float in open water until they hatch. The **larvae** quickly move to shallow water. When the baby barracudas are about 1.2 inches (3 cm) long, they swim back out to deep water.

Barracuda larvae don't look much like adults until they're about 0.5 inch (1.3 cm) long.

FACT 17

Check out the rings on a barracuda's scales to learn its age.

Barracudas live to be about 14 years old.

To figure out how old a barracuda is, you can count the rings on its scales. Another way to figure out its age is to peer into its ear. A small part called an otolith has rings you can count, too.

Barracuda Buddies

FACT 18

Baby barracudas sometimes swim in groups numbering in the thousands.

A school of barracudas is also called a battery. Young

barracudas like to swim in batteries of hundreds or even thousands.

Adult barracudas are more likely hunt on their own, though.

FACT 19

Batteries provide safety for young barracudas.

When barracudas swim in a group, it's not just for the good company. In fact, they swim in groups for safety. When

a predator attacks, the school swims wildly so it's harder for any one fish to become dinner.

This is a battery of blackfin barracudas.

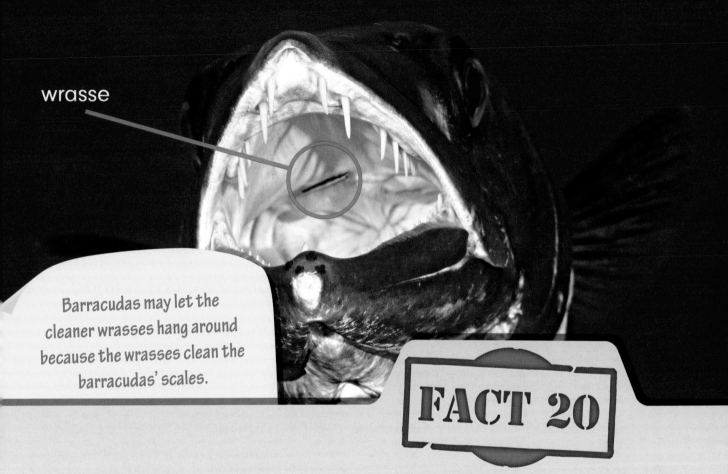

wrasse

Barracudas may let the cleaner wrasses hang around because the wrasses clean the barracudas' scales.

FACT 20

Barracudas have other finned friends, too.

Barracudas might be fierce hunters, but they sometimes hang out with other fish. Their fish friends include bar jacks, rainbow runners, and bigeye trevallies. Fish called cleaner wrasses are known to swim with barracudas, too.

Behold the Barracuda

Barracudas have such power and speed that humans have named fast vehicles after them. The US Navy has named ships after this watery fiend. From 1964 to 1974, the Chrysler car company produced a sports car called the Plymouth Barracuda.

Barracudas certainly deserve their reputation for being fast and dangerous! The fearsome barracuda is at the top of its food chain. It hardly has any predators to fear as it swims through the deep blue sea.

Glossary

caudal: near the tail

cold-blooded: having a body heat that changes with the heat around it

coral reef: a strip of coral near the surface of the water

dorsal: near the back

flexible: able to bend and move easily

larvae: fish in an early life stage that have a wormlike form

pike: a long, freshwater fish with a pointed nose and large teeth

predator: an animal that hunts other animals for food

prey: an animal that is hunted by other animals for food

temperate: not too hot or too cold

tropical: having to do with warm areas near the equator

vertebrate: an animal with a spine

For More Information

Books

Coldiron, Deborah. *Barracudas.* Edina, MN: ABDO Publishing, 2009.

Nuzzolo, Deborah. *Barracudas.* Mankato, MN: Capstone Press, 2008.

Websites

Barracuda
school.discoveryeducation.com/schooladventures/planetocean/barracuda.html
Learn more about these lean, mean, swimming machines with facts and photos.

Barracudas
www.seaworld.org/animal-info/animal-bytes/animalia/eumetazoa/coelomates/
deuterostomes/chordata/craniata/osteichthyes/perciformes/barracudas.htm
Sea World's website contains fun facts about barracudas.

Barracudas in Slow Motion
videos.howstuffworks.com/discovery/4592-barracuda-in-slow-motion-video.htm
Watch an amazing slow-motion video of a barracuda biting its prey.

Index